Hannah

THE Tooth Fairy BOOK

Text by Deborah Kovacs
Illustrations by Laura Lydecker

RUNNING PRESS
PHILADELPHIA · LONDON

9 8 7
Digit on the right indicates the number of this printing.

ISBN 1-56138-147-0

Library of Congress Cataloguing-in-Publication Number
92-53679

THE TOOTH FAIRY BOOK
was prepared and produced by Magnolia Editions Limited,
15 West 26th Street, New York, New York 10010

Editor: Karla Olson
Art Director/Designer: Jeff Batzli
Production: Karen Matsu Greenberg

Printed in China

Published by Running Press Book Publishers, 125 South Twenty-second Street,
Philadelphia, Pennsylvania 19103-4399

Contents

A Welcome from the Tooth Fairy

There are a few wonderful, exciting events in your life that show you are actually growing up—when you take your first step or say your first word. And there is another important growing-up step, one you are about to take— losing your baby teeth.

When you were born, everything about you was very small—your hands, your feet, your nose, your fingernails. Your teeth were very small, too, but they fit your little mouth. Gradually your body grew bigger and bigger, until you became the size you are today.

But your teeth didn't grow along with the rest of you. Instead, you have another set of teeth under your little ones. Now you are big enough to need these grown-up teeth, so they are pushing up, and pushing your baby teeth out. At first, your new teeth may seem a little large, but don't worry—you'll grow into them.

This book will help you celebrate and remember this important time in your life. The book begins with "The Tale of the Tooth Fairy," my story about the magical things that can happen when you lose a tooth.

In "The Wide World of Teeth" and "Tall Tooth Tales," you'll discover the many ways children around the world celebrate losing their teeth and the funny things some people believe about teeth. You'll laugh at the tooth riddles and jokes and enjoy some very silly poems.

At the end of this book, you can keep your tooth history by filling in "My Own Tooth Tale." Later you'll have fun looking back at your story as you grow up and enjoy other magical days.

When you lose a tooth, put it in the beautiful tooth pouch included with this book, and place the pouch under your pillow. When you fall asleep, make a wish, and maybe—just maybe—I will take **you** on a trip to the stars.

THE Tale OF THE Tooth Fairy

In Fairyland, far beyond the rainbow, there is a magical place where the Growing-Up Fairies live. Two of these are the First-Step Fairy and the First-Word Fairy. The busiest of all, though, is the Tooth Fairy, for she visits children each time one of their baby teeth falls out.

The Tooth Fairy collects baby teeth to make the stars that sparkle in the sky. It takes many teeth to make a star, and the Tooth Fairy has been collecting children's baby teeth for a long, long time. (You can tell by trying to count all the stars at night.)

Each time a child loses a tooth, the Tooth Fairy flies down from Fairyland in a shower of golden sparkles. She takes the tooth from its pouch hidden under the child's pillow, and leaves a gift in its place.

The first time a child loses a tooth, something extra-special happens. Let's join Jesse as he celebrates his first lost tooth.

For what seemed like forever, Jesse longed to lose a tooth. One of Jesse's teeth started wiggling months ago. But though the tooth got looser and looser, it just would not fall out.

"This tooth is never coming out," sighed Jesse, giving it still another wiggle and twist. All day long, Jesse wiggled and wiggled the tooth. Then he wiggled some more.

Finally, out it popped. "Wow!" shouted Jesse. "I lost a tooth!"

He held the tooth in his hand. It was small, smooth, shiny, and white as a pearl. "I can't believe it," Jesse cheered. He ran his tongue over the empty space in his mouth where his tooth had been.

On Jesse's last birthday, his mother had given him a special pouch just to hold his baby teeth. "When you lose a tooth, put it in this pouch," his mother said, smiling. "I've heard that there's a Tooth Fairy who sometimes trades a gift for a tooth."

Jesse took his tooth pouch from its hiding place and put his tooth inside.

When he went to bed that night, he slipped the pouch under his pillow. "I hope the Tooth Fairy pays me a visit," thought Jesse.

Far away in Fairyland, a bright green light blinked on
a huge map of the world. "Someone's lost a tooth!" the
Tooth Fairy exclaimed to the other Growing-Up Fairies.
"It's a first tooth! Let's get ready to celebrate!" In Fairyland,
losing a first tooth is a very special event. It means someone
is really growing up.

Without pausing for a second, the Tooth Fairy sped to earth in a shower of golden sparkles and hovered at Jesse's bedside. She gently slipped the pouch from under the pillow, and then wrapped Jesse in her magic flying blanket.

The Tooth Fairy flew quickly through the clear, starry night, carrying Jesse so gently that he did not wake up.

When they arrived in Fairyland, the Tooth Fairy kissed Jesse's forehead. "Wake up, Jesse," she whispered. Jesse's eyes opened wide, for he was in the most dazzling place he had ever seen. Everything glittered with fairy dust. All the Growing-Up Fairies were there, dressed in their finest clothes, and a long banquet table was filled with Jesse's favorite foods. (In the fairyland of dreams, children can eat just what they want.)

CONGRATULATIONS, JESSE!
read a big banner floating in the air.

The Tooth Fairy put a shiny gold crown on Jesse's head, took his hand, and led him to a big throne at the head of the table. "This is your place because you're our guest of honor," she said with a warm smile.

After the banquet, Jesse and the fairies played, danced, and sang the night away.

Overhead, a huge comet suddenly flashed by, its long tail streaking behind it. "Would you like to take a ride with me?" asked the Tooth Fairy. Jesse took the Fairy's outstretched hand. Together, they zoomed through space on the tail of the comet until they came to a place in the sky that was completely dark. The Tooth Fairy handed Jesse his pouch. "Set your tooth free," she whispered.

Jesse shook out the pouch. The tooth flew into the sky, into an empty spot where it remained, twinkling. "A new star has been born," the Tooth Fairy told Jesse. "Every tooth you lose will join this star, your star, making it shine brighter and brighter." Then the Tooth Fairy waved at the star and called, "Goodbye, little tooth. May a strong, new tooth grow in your place."

The comet carried Jesse and the Tooth Fairy back to the sky above Jesse's house. They let go and glided gently onto Jesse's bed. The Tooth Fairy put a shiny coin in Jesse's pouch and placed it under his pillow.

"See you next tooth!" whispered the Tooth Fairy, to an already sleeping Jesse, as she disappeared in a shower of glittering sparkles.

The second Jesse woke up the next morning, he remembered the night's adventure. "Was it all a dream?" he wondered. He reached under his pillow. There was the beautiful velvet pouch. Nestled inside was a shiny coin. And in the empty space in Jesse's mouth, a permanent tooth had already begun to poke up!

The Wide World of Teeth

Children all over the world celebrate in many different ways when their teeth fall out.

In North America, children who put lost teeth under their pillows sometimes find a note from the Tooth Fairy as well as a coin.

In many countries, parents teach their children to pretend to offer their baby teeth to mice. They hope the mouse will give back a permanent tooth as strong as the mouse's.

On the islands near New Guinea children throw their teeth up onto the roof for the mice. In Germany and Mexico they put the teeth in a mouse's hole.

Yugoslavian children throw their teeth onto the roof and call to any crow that is nearby, "Oh, dear crow, here is a tooth of bone. Take it and give me a tooth of iron instead, so that I can chew beans and crunch dry biscuits."

Ukrainian children throw their baby teeth backward over their heads onto the roof, saying: "Mouse, mouse, here is a tooth of bone, give me one of iron."

Saudi Arabian children throw their baby teeth to the sun, saying: "Give me a better one for it."

Cherokees know that beavers have very strong teeth. Cherokee children who lose teeth run all around the outside of the house with them, repeating four times: "Beaver, put a new tooth into my jaw." Then the children throw the teeth up onto the roof.

Long ago in England, children went into the woods and threw their teeth over their right shoulders. They believed that when they returned later to the spot, a treasure would be waiting.

In Japan, children throw their baby teeth into rainbarrels, saying, "My teeth are weak, so I trade them for those of the devil."

23

Tall Tooth Tales

Do you believe in these superstitions? Many people do.

If you can keep your tongue out of the hole where a tooth is missing (this is almost impossible to do), a gold tooth will grow in its place.

If a quarter can be placed in the space between your teeth, you'll be rich.

If your teeth are set far apart, you may take long journeys or be able to sing a fine tune. But if your teeth are close together, you'll live with your mother—always.

If your mother or father puts your first lost tooth in a hole in a willow tree and then plugs up the hole, you'll never get a toothache—ever.

You'd better not throw your tooth outdoors. If a rabbit runs over it, your next tooth will be a rabbit's tooth. If a dog or a rat finds it, you will get a dog or a rat tooth.

Tooth Trivia:
Sayings, Riddles, and Poems

"A diamond is not as precious as a tooth."

Cervantes, DON QUIXOTE

"The best of friends fall out, and so his teeth had done so years ago."

Thomas Hood, A TRUE STORY

"An aching tooth is better out than in. To lose a rotten member is a gain."

Richard Baxter, HYPOCRISY

"Hot things, sharp things,
sweet things, cold things,
All rot the teeth and make
them look like olde things."

Benjamin Franklin,
POOR RICHARD'S ALMANACK

"If you cannot bite, never
show your teeth."

John Ray, ENGLISH PROVERBS

MISLAID FALSE TEETH

There once was an old man
     named Keith,
Who mislaid his pair of
     false teeth,
Laid them down on a chair,
Forgot they were there,
Sat down and was bitten
     beneath.

Toothy Riddles

Knock, knock
    Who's there?
Fang.
    Fang who?
Fang you very much.

What kind of teeth can you
buy for a dollar?
    Buck teeth.

What comes out at night
and goes, "Flap, flap, flap,
OUCH!"
    *A vampire with a sore
tooth.*

28

Why are false teeth like stars?

Because they come out at night.

What has teeth but no mouth?

A saw.

What is the best thing to put into a pie?

Your teeth.

What is worse than brushing a shark's tooth?

Removing its tonsils.

DENTIST: I see you've lost your two front teeth.
ALBERT: *No, I haven't. I have them in my pocket.*

What helps keep your teeth together?

Toothpaste.

My Own Tooth Tale by

_____

(NAME)

Write down when, where, and how you lost your teeth. Then write the dates of all your lost teeth on the Tooth Map.

This is me before I lost any teeth.

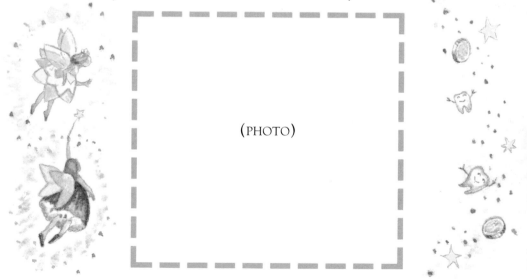

(PHOTO)

I first noticed a loose tooth in my mouth on
4-27 03 day _April_ month _2003_ year, when I
was __7__ years old.

I lost my **first** tooth on ▲ day_____month_____year,
when I was _____ years old.

This is how I lost it: _____

_____

_____

_____

This is how I felt:_____

_____

_____

_____

31

This is what everybody said:

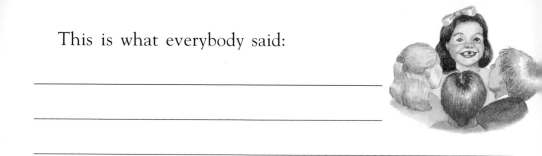

_____

_____

_____

This is what I looked like after I lost my **first** tooth.

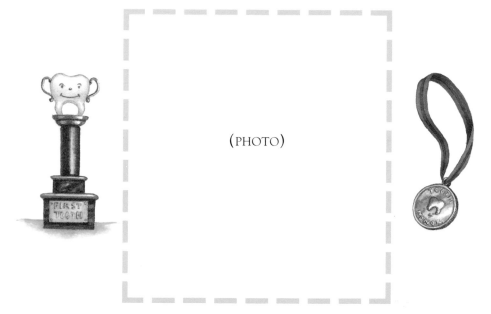

(PHOTO)

This is how I looked after I lost my **front** tooth.

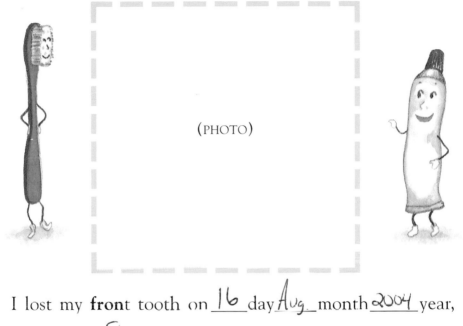

(PHOTO)

I lost my **front** tooth on _16_ day _Aug_ month _2004_ year, when I was _8_ years old.

This is where I was when it came out: _eating lunch_ _while at Alafia Elementary - bit into_ _a carrott and after chewing a few_ _times it fell out_

33

This is how I lost it: <u>Chewing a</u>
<u>carrott</u>
_____

This is how I felt:_____
_____
_____
_____
_____

This is what everybody said:_____
_____
_____
_____

Tooth Map

Here is a map of my teeth and when I lost each of them.

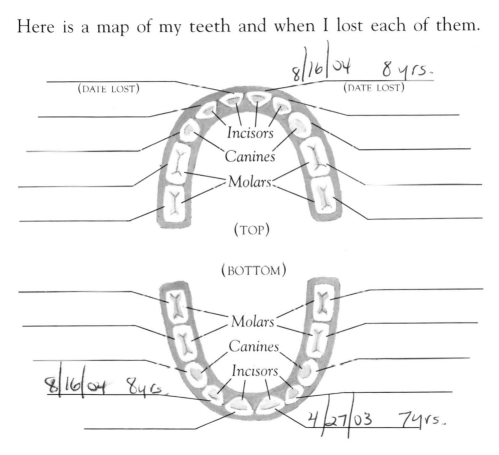

8/16/04 8 yrs.

(DATE LOST)   (DATE LOST)

Incisors

Canines

Molars

(TOP)

(BOTTOM)

Molars

Canines

Incisors

8/16/04 8 yrs.

4/27/03 7 yrs.

35

Farewell, Tooth

For oh so long I waited,
For a tooth that I could
    wiggle.
When at last the moment
    came,
I gave it quite a jiggle.

That tooth was very
    stubborn,
It made me want to pout!
Though day by day it
    looser grew,
It just would not fall out.

Then one fine day my
    auntie said,
"An apple's what you need."
I took one bite. Out popped
    my tooth.
My aunt was right, indeed!

I screamed with joy. I was
    so proud!
I didn't feel a pain.
"I'll rinse it off!" I thought.
Then my tooth fell down
    the drain!

No tooth beneath my
    pillow!
What was I going to do?
No tooth, no Fairy, so I
    thought.
No quarter...oh, boohoo!

Because there was no tooth
    to leave,
I left a note instead.
Next day I found a letter.
I opened it and read:

"Was that your tooth that
    washed away?
I heard it on Tooth News.
No matter! For I've got it
    now.
A tooth is hard to lose.

"I dove into the drain and
    then
I found the little thing.
I put it in my tooth pouch
And tied it with a string.

"So here's your quarter with
    my thanks,
Your tooth I'm glad to gain.
But next time, when you
    lose a tooth,
Be sure to shut the drain."

38